OUR SOLAR SYSTEM
THE ASTEROID BELT

by Yvette LaPierre

San Diego, CA

© 2023 BrightPoint Press
an imprint of ReferencePoint Press, Inc.
Printed in the United States

For more information, contact:
BrightPoint Press
PO Box 27779
San Diego, CA 92198
www.BrightPointPress.com

ALL RIGHTS RESERVED.

No part of this work covered by the copyright hereon may be reproduced or used in any form or by any means—graphic, electronic, or mechanical, including photocopying, recording, taping, web distribution, or information storage retrieval systems—without the written permission of the publisher.

LIBRARY OF CONGRESS CATALOGING-IN-PUBLICATION DATA

Name: LaPierre, Yvette, author.
Title: The asteroid belt / by Yvette LaPierre.
Description: San Diego, CA: ReferencePoint Press, Inc., 2023 | Series: Our Solar System | Audience: Grade 10 to 12 | Includes bibliographical references and index.
Identifiers: ISBN: 9781678204020 (hardcover) | ISBN: 9781678204037 (eBook)
The complete Library of Congress record is available at www.loc.gov.

CONTENTS

AT A GLANCE	4

INTRODUCTION	6
SAFE TRAVELS	

CHAPTER ONE	12
SPACE RUBBLE	

CHAPTER TWO	24
ASTEROID BELT BEGINNINGS	

CHAPTER THREE	32
DISCOVERY AND EXPLORATION	

CHAPTER FOUR	44
COLLIDING ASTEROIDS	

Glossary	58
Source Notes	59
For Further Research	60
Index	62
Image Credits	63
About the Author	64

AT A GLANCE

- The asteroid belt is a donut-shaped area of space between the orbits of Jupiter and Mars.

- The asteroid belt contains millions of rocky bodies called asteroids.

- Asteroids are the pieces that were left over when planets formed billions of years ago.

- The bodies in the asteroid belt range in size from tiny particles of dust to dwarf planets.

- The largest body in the asteroid belt is the dwarf planet Ceres.

- Astronomers discovered Ceres in 1801. They considered it an asteroid. It was later reclassified as a dwarf planet.

- The asteroid belt is mostly empty space.

- In 2001, a spacecraft landed on an asteroid for the first time.

- Asteroids are sometimes knocked out of the asteroid belt. Those that fall to Earth are called meteorites.

- Large asteroids could pose a threat to Earth. Scientists and engineers are studying ways to prevent dangerous impacts from happening.

INTRODUCTION

SAFE TRAVELS

The spacecraft flew past the **orbit** of Mars. It headed into the asteroid belt. From afar, this area looks like a donut-shaped cloud. Science fiction films portray the belt as packed with rocks. But the real spacecraft safely steered through it. The asteroid belt contains millions of objects, but space is so vast that the belt is not crowded. It is mostly empty space. In fact, the average distance between large asteroids is hundreds of thousands of miles.

Some spacecraft visit asteroids to collect samples for scientists to study.

The spacecraft flew close enough to take photos of one odd-shaped rock. It surveyed the asteroid's pitted, cratered surface. It measured its shape and size. It even landed on the asteroid to take samples. The spacecraft was also looking for evidence of water. Studying asteroids can help scientists learn more about the history of the **solar system**.

THE ASTEROID BELT

The solar system has many millions of asteroids. Between Mars and Jupiter is an oval of space where many of these space

The asteroid belt is found between the orbits of Mars and Jupiter.

rocks orbit the Sun. This region is known as the asteroid belt.

Asteroids often have irregular shapes. A few of the largest ones are shaped more like a ball. Most asteroids are rocky, but some are made of metals. They range in size. Some are tiny pebbles. Others are many miles across. Some even have their own moons. Other asteroids are just loose piles of rubble or dust. Asteroids orbit the Sun. But they are too small to be considered **planets**.

Asteroids sometimes leave their orbits. They may bump into each other. This can knock away small pieces. A larger body's **gravity** may fling the pieces out of the belt. This can send them on a collision course with a planet. When asteroids land on Earth, they are called meteorites. Scientists study meteorites to see what they are made of.

Studying meteorites can help scientists learn more about asteroids.

They send spacecraft to investigate the asteroid belt. Asteroids hold important clues about the early solar system. They can help us understand how planets formed.

1
SPACE RUBBLE

Asteroids are space rubble left over after the solar system formed about 4.6 billion years ago. Most orbit the Sun in the asteroid belt between Mars and Jupiter. "This is the cool place in our solar system where all the small bodies go," says **astronomer** William Bottke.[1]

The asteroid belt is also known as the main belt. This distinguishes it from other collections of asteroids. The Kuiper belt is beyond the orbit of Neptune. The Trojan asteroids are found near Jupiter.

Gravity pulls together gas and dust to form planets. The leftover material may form asteroids.

To measure distances in the solar system, scientists use astronomical units (AU). One AU is the average distance from Earth to the Sun. This is about 93 million miles (150 million km). The main belt starts about 2 AU from the Sun. It extends outward for about 1 AU. The rocky planets, including Earth, are nearer to the Sun. The giant gas planets are beyond the main belt.

KUIPER BELT

The Kuiper belt contains millions of icy objects. Hundreds of thousands are larger than 62 miles (100 km) across. The biggest is the **dwarf planet** Pluto. Pluto is about 1,400 miles (2,380 km) wide. It has about fourteen times more **mass** than Ceres.

SPACE ROCKS

The exact number of asteroids in the belt is unknown. Scientists estimate that there are millions of them. More than 1 million are larger than 0.6 miles (1 km) wide. Astronomers have found more than 200 that are larger than 60 miles (100 km) across. The largest body in the asteroid belt is Ceres. It is nearly 600 miles (950 km) wide. Asteroids orbit the Sun just as Earth and the other planets do. More than 150 even have their own tiny moons.

Millions of asteroids may seem like a lot. But their combined mass doesn't add

Asteroids come in a range of shapes and sizes.

up to much. Put together, all the main belt's asteroids have a mass that is about 4 percent of the Moon's.

Most asteroids look like irregular-shaped rocks. This is because of their small size. Without much mass, they don't have strong gravity. As a result, gravity can't pull them into a round shape. Only a few of the largest asteroids are round. The surfaces of asteroids are pitted. This results from many small collisions over time.

ASTEROID TYPES

The asteroid belt contains three kinds of asteroids. C-type, or carbon-rich, are the most common. They are found mostly in the outer part of the belt. This region is closest to Jupiter. C-type asteroids are dark in color. Scientists think they are made of clay and **silicate** rocks. These asteroids are some of the oldest objects in the solar system.

S-type asteroids are the second type. These are stony asteroids. They contain silicate materials and some metals. They are greenish and reddish in color. Stony asteroids are found mostly in the inner part of the belt near Mars.

Third are M-type asteroids. These asteroids are metallic. They are a reddish color. They appear to be made of nickel and iron. These are the least common asteroids. They are found in the middle part of the belt.

A large asteroid called Psyche is an M-type asteroid.

CERES

Ceres is the largest object in the main belt. It was discovered in 1801. Ceres is about the size of Australia. It is one-quarter as wide as Earth's Moon. The mass of Ceres

Ceres is by far the largest object in the asteroid belt.

accounts for nearly a third of all the mass in the belt.

Unlike most asteroids, Ceres is round. It has lots of big craters on its surface.

WHERE IS THE ASTEROID BELT?

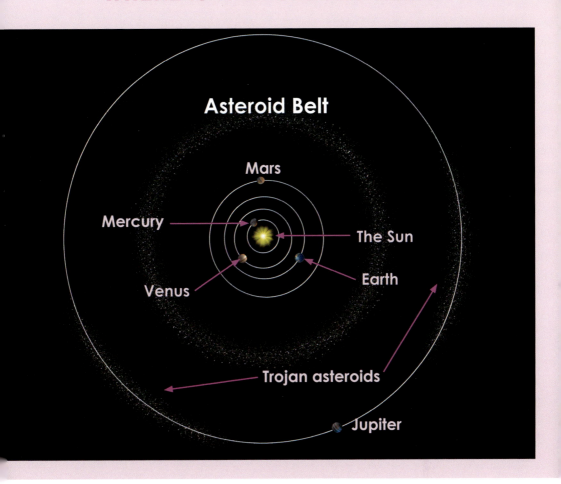

The asteroid belt is the donut-shaped area between Mars and Jupiter where asteroids orbit the Sun. It divides the four rocky planets nearest to the Sun from the four big gas planets that are farthest away.

Scientists think there is an ocean of ice under its surface.

Ceres is named for the Roman goddess of farming.

Ceres was originally called an asteroid. But it is much larger than other asteroids. In 2006, scientists reclassified it as a dwarf planet. Ceres is one of five dwarf planets. It is the only one in the inner solar system. It was the first dwarf planet to be visited by a spacecraft. This mission arrived in 2015.

2
ASTEROID BELT BEGINNINGS

For the first few million years of our solar system, the planets were forming. Astronomer William Bottke notes, "The solar system of today looks very different from the way it looked 4.5 billion years ago."[2] As planets formed, they scattered smaller objects out of the way. Sometimes these new planets crashed into each other. That's how scientists once thought the asteroid belt formed. They believed there must have been a big planet in the area. They thought collisions blasted it to pieces. This formed the asteroid belt.

The early solar system was a violent place with many collisions.

But there were several problems with this explanation. First, it would take too much energy to destroy an entire planet. Second, the amount of material in the belt wouldn't add up to a planet. And last, astronomers found that asteroids and meteorites are made from a variety of materials. That means they couldn't have all come from one planet.

PIECES OF PLANETS

Most astronomers now think the asteroid belt contains the leftover pieces from when the planets formed. Gravity pulled larger

Jupiter's powerful gravity likely influenced the formation of the asteroid belt.

clumps of material together. This formed the solar system's planets. But some smaller pieces did not join these large clumps. They scattered into the solar system.

Many ended up in orbits between Jupiter and Mars.

Jupiter is huge. It has a strong gravitational pull. Mars is much smaller. Its pull is much weaker. The asteroids between them get pulled around and crash into each other. Many astronomers think this stopped the asteroids from forming larger bodies. Instead, they have remained millions of small, separate rocks. They have been orbiting the Sun since the early days of the solar system.

A NEW THEORY

Some scientists now think that explanation is too simple. They believe the asteroid belt was once bigger than it is now. It may have had as much mass as Earth. According to this theory, Jupiter formed a few million years before Saturn. The Sun's gravity pulled Jupiter inward toward the

JUPITER'S ASTEROIDS

Jupiter is the biggest planet in the solar system. It has many moons and two swarms of asteroids. These asteroids are called the Trojans. In October 2021, the US space agency launched the first mission to study Jupiter's asteroids. The *Lucy* spacecraft will visit both the main belt and the Trojans.

The Hubble Space Telescope has helped scientists learn more about the asteroid belt's history.

Sun. As Jupiter moved through the belt, it scattered some of the asteroids. Then Saturn formed. Its mass pulled Jupiter back through the belt again. More asteroids flew out of the belt. Many of them may have struck the inner planets.

3
DISCOVERY AND EXPLORATION

By the 1700s, astronomers had studied the motions of Mercury, Venus, Earth, Mars, Jupiter, and Saturn. They observed the planets' orbits. They found that the spacing between planets followed a predictable pattern. But there was one exception. There appeared to be a gap between the orbits of Mars and Jupiter. It seemed there should be a planet there, but there wasn't.

ASTEROID DISCOVERY

In 1801, Italian astronomer Giuseppe Piazzi was observing the sky and making a map

Giuseppe Piazzi discovered Ceres in 1801.

Scientists discovered many more large objects in the asteroid belt over time.

of the stars. He discovered a large object between Mars and Jupiter. This object was soon named Ceres.

Other astronomers began to find more objects in the same area. They looked like stars or comets. But they moved more like planets. Eventually, scientists put them in their own category. They called them asteroids. This comes from the Greek for "star-like."

By the 1850s, the term *asteroid* was in common use. Astronomers began to call the gap between Mars and Jupiter the asteroid belt. Better technology made it easier to discover more asteroids. Scientists had identified 1,000 asteroids in the belt by 1921. By 1981, they had found 10,000 asteroids. And by the year 2000, they had found 100,000 of them.

This number continued to grow. In 2022, the known asteroid count was over

1 million. Astronomers continue to scan space and find more.

EXPLORING ASTEROIDS

Scientists are very interested in what asteroids are made of and how they came to be. Understanding asteroids will help them learn how the solar system formed. Scientists study the asteroids that land on Earth as meteorites. The National Aeronautics and Space Administration (NASA) has also sent probes to visit asteroids in space. NASA is the US national space agency.

Because the asteroid belt is mostly empty space, spacecraft can fly safely through it. *Pioneer 10* was the first to pass through the belt. It crossed through in 1972 and 1973. It was on a mission to Jupiter. Since then, several other ships have journeyed through the belt.

In 2001, a spacecraft landed on an asteroid for the first time. NASA's

ASTEROID NAMES

The astronomer who first finds an asteroid gets to name it. Some scientists name asteroids after their pets. Others name them after favorite musicians. Seven asteroids were named in memory of the astronauts who were killed in the Space Shuttle *Columbia* disaster in 2003.

An illustration shows NEAR arriving at Eros.

NEAR spacecraft touched down on the asteroid Eros. Eros was 196 million miles (315 million km) away from Earth at the time.

Before landing, *NEAR* circled Eros. It took close-up photos of its surface. It measured Eros's size and shape. Eros has craters and a long ridge on its surface. It is an S-type asteroid. This makes it similar to most asteroids found in the asteroid belt. It is not in the belt, though. It orbits between Mars and Earth. It may be a fragment from asteroids that collided in the main belt millions of years ago.

In 2018, NASA sent the *OSIRIS-REx* spacecraft to the asteroid Bennu. Bennu is shaped like a spinning top. It is about one-third of a mile (0.5 km) across. That's a bit wider than the Empire State Building is tall. It appears to be made from materials dating to the early solar system. Scientists think it may contain materials like those that started life on Earth.

Scientists put OSIRIS-REx through many tests before launch.

Bennu is likely a piece that was broken off a larger asteroid in the main belt. It has since drifted out of the belt and closer to Earth. It's about 180 million miles (290 million km) away.

OSIRIS-REx did not travel directly to Bennu. After leaving Earth, it orbited the Sun once. Then it swung past Earth again. The planet's gravity changed the spacecraft's speed and angle. This put it on a path to reach Bennu.

In July 2020, two years after leaving Earth, *OSIRIS-REx* flew close enough to collect dirt and rocks from Bennu's surface. The spacecraft headed home with the samples in May 2021. A capsule containing bits of Bennu was planned to reach Earth in 2023. These samples would contain valuable information about the asteroid. They would also teach astronomers more than they can learn from meteorites.

OSIRIS-REx took this photo of Bennu's surface as it reached out to grab a sample.

Scientist Dante Lauretta explains, "We're going to get a much better understanding of the most fragile materials that are on these asteroids and in space, that don't survive passage to the Earth's atmosphere."[3]

Scientists explore asteroids to learn more about the formation of the solar system.

They are also interested in how asteroids can be used. Asteroids contain metals and minerals that people might be able to mine. The materials could be turned into building materials or rocket fuel. Or the metals could be sent back to Earth. It's even possible that astronauts could build space stations on larger asteroids one day.

ASTEROID MINING

NASA has estimated that all the metal in the asteroid belt is worth $700 quintillion. That's 700 followed by 18 zeros. That would be enough money for every person on Earth to have $100 billion. However, actually reaching those asteroids and mining them would be extremely expensive.

4
COLLIDING ASTEROIDS

Collisions between asteroids in the main belt are common. These millions of space rocks orbit the Sun together. Sometimes they tumble and knock into each other. These collisions can break bits off an asteroid. That's why many larger asteroids have pits and craters on their surfaces. When small asteroids are hit by larger ones, they may be reduced to tiny pieces.

Sometimes a big collision can smash an asteroid into smaller asteroids. All these

Huge craters are evidence of collisions in an asteroid's past.

asteroids then belong to one family. Asteroid families are made of similar material and have similar orbits. The largest asteroid in the belt that belongs to a family is Vesta. It is the second-largest object in the belt. Only the dwarf planet Ceres is larger. The Vesta family of asteroids probably formed about a billion years ago. A massive impact broke off a big chunk of the original Vesta asteroid. It made a crater 310 miles (500 km) wide on Vesta's surface.

TRAVELING ASTEROIDS

Sometimes collisions can knock an asteroid out of its orbit. The gravity of Jupiter or other planets can hurl the asteroid out of the belt. The traveling asteroid may smash into a planet. All planets in the solar system have

FIREBALL!

An asteroid lit up the sky above a city in Russia on a February morning in 2013. It created a fireball that exploded 18.4 miles (29.7 km) above the city of Chelyabinsk. The explosion shattered windows for miles and injured more than a thousand people. Scientists believe the asteroid was about the size of a six-story building.

been struck by asteroids. These impacts have changed the surfaces of planets.

Asteroids have slammed into Earth ever since it formed about 4.6 billion years ago. Small pea-sized asteroids burn up high in the atmosphere. Larger asteroids the size of boulders explode brightly. These are called fireballs. Asteroids as big as cars may reach the ground as meteorites. NASA reports that one or two big meteorites enter Earth's atmosphere each year.

Most meteorites are harmless. Some impacts can even be helpful. Scientists think that asteroids may have brought organic

Small asteroids burn up harmlessly in the atmosphere, appearing as shooting stars.

compounds to Earth early in its history. But someday a huge asteroid could hit Earth. This would cause widespread damage. Such a disaster has happened in the past. Scientists believe an impact 66 million years ago killed off the dinosaurs.

NEAR-EARTH ASTEROIDS

Astronomers don't worry too much about asteroids in the belt and beyond. They orbit far from Earth. But many asteroids orbit outside the belt. The ones that approach Earth are called near-Earth asteroids. Some near-Earth asteroids circle the Sun between Earth and Mars. Others only occasionally cross Earth's orbit. Still others are completely within Earth's orbit. By October 2021, scientists had identified more than 27,000 near-Earth asteroids.

Hundreds of these asteroids are considered potentially hazardous.

A large asteroid impact could devastate a region or even the whole planet.

This means their orbits come close to Earth and they are big enough to cause a disaster. If a large asteroid hit a city, it could kill many people. A big meteorite strike

Astronomers use ground-based telescopes to watch out for nearby asteroids.

to the ocean could create giant waves.

Coastal areas could be wiped out.

Very large asteroids could have worldwide effects. An asteroid more than a quarter-mile wide could cause a global disaster. It would throw dust into the atmosphere. This could block out the Sun for a long time. It would create dark, winter-like conditions around the world.

PLANETARY DEFENSE

Currently, Earth is not threatened by a large asteroid. But scientists keep their eyes on space, just in case. An asteroid impact is one type of natural disaster that humans may be able to prevent.

NASA has a group called the Planetary Defense Coordination Office. Scientists

Space-based telescopes help scientists spot potentially dangerous asteroids.

there watch near-Earth asteroids. They use radar to monitor these objects. Radar signals can tell scientists the size, shape, and orbit of asteroids. Scientists can find out if these objects are headed for Earth. Advance warning of an impact will be important. Science TV show host Bill Nye says, "The first step toward protecting our planet is to find and track the swarm of space rocks that cross orbits with Earth."[4]

If an asteroid threat is found early, scientists may have a long time to prepare. There may be years or even decades of warning. NASA isn't waiting, though. The agency is developing technologies to protect Earth. One way is to change the course of an asteroid. In November 2021, NASA launched a mission to test this. This is the *Double Asteroid Redirection Test* (*DART*) mission.

The *DART* spacecraft weighs 1,200 pounds (544 kg). It is the size of a refrigerator. It flew around the Sun on its way to an asteroid. Scientists planned to slam the spacecraft into the asteroid at 15,000 miles per hour (24,140 kmh). Then they would watch to see how the asteroid's path changed. Before impact, *DART* would release a smaller spacecraft. It would take pictures of the collision. This test was important. NASA scientist Lindley Johnson says, "We don't want to be flying an untested capability when we're trying to save a population on the Earth's surface."[5]

The DART mission's goal is to test a way of changing an asteroid's orbit.

Discoveries about asteroids have helped unlock mysteries of the early solar system. At the same time, studying asteroids has shown how they could threaten Earth. These space rocks are some of the most fascinating objects in our solar system.

GLOSSARY

astronomer

a scientist who studies stars, planets, and space

dwarf planet

an object in space that meets all the criteria of a planet except that it is not big enough to clear debris from its orbit

gravity

the natural force that causes physical things to move toward each other

mass

the amount of physical matter that an object contains

orbit

a circular path that an object takes when traveling around the Sun or a planet

planets

an object that orbits the Sun, is round, and has enough mass to clear other objects from its orbit

silicate

material found throughout the solar system that is made up of silicon, oxygen, and a least one metal

solar system

the Sun and everything that orbits around it, including planets, moons, asteroids, and comets

SOURCE NOTES

CHAPTER ONE: SPACE RUBBLE

1. Quoted in Joshua Rapp Learn, "The Asteroid Belt: Wreckage of a Destroyed Planet or Something Else?" *Discover*, March 9, 2021. www.astronomy.com.

CHAPTER TWO: ASTEROID BELT BEGINNINGS

2. Quoted in Learn, "The Asteroid Belt."

CHAPTER THREE: DISCOVERY AND EXPLORATION

3. Quoted in Kenneth Chang, "Bye Bye, Bennu," *New York Times*, May 10, 2021. www.nytimes.com.

CHAPTER FOUR: COLLIDING ASTEROIDS

4. Quoted in Glenn Chaple, "Asteroid Awareness," *Astronomy*, June 2015, vol. 43, issue 6, p. 14.

5. Quoted in Joey Roulette, "NASA Launches New Mission: Crash into Asteroid, Defend Planet Earth," *New York Times*, November 24, 2021. www.nytimes.com.

FOR FURTHER RESEARCH

BOOKS

Anne Jankéliowitch, *Solar System*. Cambridge, MA: Barefoot Books, 2019.

Kevin Kurtz, *Comets and Asteroids in Action*. Minneapolis, MN: Lerner Publications, 2020.

Gail Terp, *Pluto and the Dwarf Planets*. San Diego, CA: BrightPoint Press, 2023.

INTERNET SOURCES

"Arthur Ross Hall of Meteorites," *American Museum of Natural History*, n.d. www.amnh.org.

"Episode 11—We Asked a NASA Scientist: What If an Asteroid Were Going to Hit Earth?" *NASA*, October 25, 2021. www.nasa.gov.

"NASA's Next-Generation Asteroid Impact Monitoring System Goes Online," *NASA*, December 6, 2021. www.nasa.gov.

WEBSITES

DK FindOut: Solar System
www.dkfindout.com/us/space/solar-system

This website features information about all the major objects in the solar system. It also includes a solar system quiz.

NASA: Solar System
https://science.nasa.gov/solar-system

NASA's solar system website covers the observation and discovery of all the solar system's planetary bodies, including asteroids.

Smithsonian National Air and Space Museum: Exploring the Planets
https://airandspace.si.edu/exhibitions/exploring-the-planets/online/solar-system

This website features pictures and key facts about the objects in our solar system, as well as missions that have visited those objects.

INDEX

asteroid impacts, 48–53
asteroid mining, 43
asteroid sizes, 10, 15–16
asteroid types
    C-type, 17–18
    M-type, 18
    S-type, 18, 38
astronomers, 12, 15, 24, 26–28, 32–36, 37, 41, 50

Bennu, 39–42
Bottke, William, 12, 24

Ceres, 14, 15, 19–23, 34, 46
Chelyabinsk, Russia, 47

discovery, 33–36
Double Asteroid Redirection Test (DART), 55–56

Eros, 38

formation, 12, 24–31

Johnson, Lindley, 56
Jupiter, 8, 12, 13, 17, 21, 28, 29–31, 32–35, 37, 47

Kuiper belt, 13, 14

Lauretta, Dante, 42
Lucy, 29

Mars, 6, 8, 12, 18, 21, 28, 32–35, 39, 50
meteorites, 10, 26, 36, 41, 48, 51

NEAR, 38
near-Earth asteroids, 50–52
Nye, Bill, 55

OSIRIS-REx, 39–41

Piazzi, Giuseppe, 33–34
Pioneer 10, 37
Planetary Defense Coordination Office, 53

Sun, 9, 10, 12, 14, 15, 21, 28, 29–31, 41, 44, 50, 53, 56

Trojan asteroids, 13, 21, 29

Vesta, 46

IMAGE CREDITS

Cover: © 24K Production/Shutterstock Images
5: © Johan Swanepoel/Shutterstock Images
7: © Goddard/NASA/Wikimedia
9: © Andrea Danti/Shutterstock Images
11: © Mikhail Sh/Shutterstock Images
13: © Jurik Peter/Shutterstock Images
16: © Nazarii Neshcherenskyi/Shutterstock Images
19: © ASU/JPL-Caltech/NASA
20: © UCLA/MPS/DLR/IDA/JPL-Caltech/NASA
21: © Claus Lunau/Science Source
22: © Luis Pizarro Ruiz/Shutterstock Images
25: © Pavel Gabzdyl/Shutterstock Images
27: © Josh Imerbin/Shutterstock Images
30: © JPL/NASA
33: © Science Source
34: © Jurik Peter/Shutterstock Images
38: © JPL/NASA
40: © Glenn Benson/KSC/NASA
42: © University of Arizona/Goddard/NASA/Wikimedia
45: © UCLA/MPS/DLR/IDA/JPL-Caltech/NASA
49: © Paulista/Shutterstock Images
51: © Andrzej Puchta/Shutterstock Images
52: © Belish/Shutterstock Images
54: © JPL-Caltech/NASA/Wikimedia
57: © Johns Hopkins APL/NASA/Wikimedia

ABOUT THE AUTHOR

Yvette LaPierre lives in North Dakota with her family. Her day job is academic adviser for the Indians Into Medicine program at the University of North Dakota School of Medicine and Health Sciences. She is the author of more than twenty nonfiction books for young readers.